Principle Solutions

SERVICE

AWARENESS

PERSEVERANCE

DISCIPLINE

FORGIVENESS

HUMILITY

WILLINGNESS

INTEGRITY

COURAGE

FAITH

HOPE

HONESTY

BY
JOHN CASEY

Acknowledgements

Another Great Tool for the Recovering Alcoholic..............

Ken Jones writes; John Casey is a sober man. That does not mean he is just not drinking alcohol. It means he has learned to live a sober lifestyle, with morals, values, beliefs and principles for living. He has taken what he has learned about sobriety and recovery and has put that knowledge and experience into a book.

This book is his attempt at helping us find out how he is enjoying life through the twelve principles. He shows us how to deal with situations without picking up a drink. John talks about the stumbling blocks that we go through in sobriety. He also teaches us through his own experience that drinking is not the answer nor is it the solution to life's struggles.

John discusses topics that help us deal with hard times through the twelve steps. He also shows us how to go to God for guidance instead of the drink or other destructive behaviors.

If you are looking for a tool to help you stay sober and live a lifestyle beyond your wildest dreams, then this book is for you.

Ken Jones.......
Author of; A Prodigal Return: Reflections from a Grateful Heart

Wonderful work! Any time we embark on a personal journey of spiritual growth, we give ourselves a gift. For those that may have tried the AA way of life and fell short of it's meaning, this book may help lead them back. Sometimes the BIG BOOK seems so BIG to newcomers. John's book, Principle Solutions provides a bridge to recovery that has a simple explanation for all of us.

Thank you John, for your courageous words and for sharing your life with us!

Turtle Klein........
Registered Addiction Specialist

I have been sober for over thirty two years. I have attended many meetings, workshops, conventions and seminars in my sobriety. I have also read most, if not all conference approved literature. John's book offers one of the best explanations of the principles behind the steps that I have ever heard. After completing a study of the twelve basic principles, he continues with various topics on which the recovering alcoholic is familiar with. His description of Relapse, Depression, Self-pity, Anger, Dry Drunk, Complacency and Emotional Sobriety are outstanding. All of these chapters are an excellent interpretation of the problems that any alcoholic faces. In all cases he has shown what problems that any alcoholic will occur in sobriety. In turn he has also shown how to overcome these problems with solutions through working the principles that are laid out for us.

George C........
Palm Bay, Florida

Introduction

Getting sober isn't just about stopping drinking. Drinking is only a symptom of the disease of alcoholism. It is though the first step in recovery and all it takes is a desire to stop drinking. If we just stop drinking, we are said to be dry. This is not enough if we want happiness and freedom.

Underlying alcoholism is compounded by fear and resentments from our past that we refused to deal with. It may be due to some self-justification or we may have missed it completely in our inventory. Fear is responsible for much of our negative behavior. Anger, jealousy, and resentment are only a few things that magnify our false fears. These false fears exist in a thousand different forms.

The person who just stops drinking will remain restless, agitated or simply miserable. True sobriety teaches us about living a joyous and free life. A life that is free of our fears, resentments and uncontrollable outbreaks that will usually cause more harm to any situation.

When alcoholic people finally do stop drinking, they often become emotional train wrecks. They may take up another addiction just so they won't have to look at themselves. Normal people don't usually drink more than a few drinks. Alcoholics who stop drinking and don't use the twelve steps, most likely force themselves not to drink, only to end up white-knuckling it. This is not normal behavior by any means.

Drinking to an alcoholic is like oxygen. The program of Alcoholics Anonymous is a design for living that negates the need to drink and guides us to live a balanced life. This way of life is proven by millions of people.

Various studies of those who are abstinent show they can return to productive lives in the community. This isn't true for people trying to control their drinking. More than half of them return to alcoholic drinking even after five years of abstinence. They appear to have made significant gains in their overall behavior in most cases but, those who control their drinking after a period of suffering from alcoholism don't appear to excel. They seem to do better than those who continue to drink abusively. Remember that normal people don't think about having to control their drinking.

Recovery starts by changing one's behaviors and actions. Then there will be a need for a change of playgrounds and playmates. Many that follow the lead may end up in recovery themselves. A person doesn't need to ride the garbage truck all the way to the dump either. They can get off any time they want. It is much easier though to get off before the truck dumps it's load.

What about finding our bottoms? It is said there are low bottom and high bottom alcoholics. A bottom just refers to the point where an alcoholic decides that they have had enough. They simply need to stop digging! They are tired of living the life they have been living and know it's time for a change. Many of us need to choose when we have reached a bottom. Because for a lot of us, the reality is that our bottom may be death.

For many of us it becomes a point of incomprehensible demoralization. It's that place where our best friend Mr. Booze turns on us and no longer is able to deliver us any happiness or freedom from our pain. Our out of control drinking increasingly causes us depression, anxiety and withdrawal. If we don't take certain steps after we stop drinking, then all of these feelings will continue and the end results will be as devastating as if we never stopped.

Carl Jung talked about the need for a spiritual solution. Bill Wilson called it a spiritual awakening. The Big Book of Alcoholics Anonymous tells us that it is not just a theory. "Spiritus contra spiritum." This is where the Higher Power conquers the lower power. The Holy Spirit is greater than liquid spirits. We step out of the darkness of our alcoholic suffering and into the light of a spiritual life.

The Twelve AA Principles

The Twelve Principles in relation to the Twelve Steps of Alcoholics Anonymous can sometimes be difficult to understand. Step twelve says that we need to practice these principles in all of our affairs. So it is important to know what they are and how they will help us in sobriety. The following is an effort to simplify their meanings. These guides to living are imperative for the recovering alcoholic. Learning about each of these principles will help us start to rebuild our self-esteem, self-confidence and secure our recovery. *Here are the action principles behind the Twelve Steps:*

1. **Honesty** - It is important to admit that we are alcoholic if we are to attain sobriety. If we don't completely admit defeat and surrender, we will never succeed. We must be truthful with ourselves! The alcoholic who still is drinking cannot tell the truth from a lie. When we finally get honest with ourselves, we begin the spiritual program of action.

2. **Hope** - If we are ready for a course of recovery, we must have hope for success. If we have no hope, then why should we try at all? We have not been able to stay sober on our own, so what have we got to lose? Hope comes from the desperation we feel when we enter AA. To instill hope is to realize that recovery is not just a question of trying, but rather a desire to stay sober. Seeing others recover and living happy lives free of alcohol, brings hope.

3. **Faith** - This step decides on if we are to keep going with the rest of the steps. It asks us that we step out on faith. Here we only need to be willing to believe. As we progress through the twelve steps, our hope will turn into

faith. We must begin to have faith that it will work, but we must remember that faith without works will not prevail.

4. **Courage** - To honestly look at ourselves takes a tremendous amount of courage. We will see how our behavior has become warped and how we justified our actions. We have come to the point where we take a honest assessment of ourselves. When we look at the causes, conditions and effects of our drinking behaviors, our fears can be overcome through courage.

5. **Integrity** - If we have been thorough and evaluated our shortcomings, do we now have the integrity to own up to these defects? It can be difficult to be honest and open about our past. By continuing to do the right thing even when no one is watching we gain a dose of humility.

6. **Willingness** - Now that we have completed our inventory of character and behavior, are we willing to change our defects? Are we willing to give all of them to God? Here it is important to be willing to let go of old behaviors and be willing to rely on our Higher Power.

7. **Humility** - We have seen in step five where we were selfish and self-centered. We practice being humble by realizing that we aren't the center of the universe and accept ourselves for being imperfect. To be human is to make mistakes. Hopefully we are at the point where we can readily admits our mistakes. Can we ask for help in learning how to forgive ourselves?

8. **Forgiveness** - We have prepared a list of those to whom we owe amends. Our motive is not to expect forgiveness, but to apply restitution for our wrongs. If we obtain forgiveness then that is a bonus. We must also learn not to judge others, but accept them for who they are and not who we think they should be.

9. **Discipline** - We need to continue to remove the walls

that can block our growth in sobriety. We are cleaning up our side of the street. We are learning to become accountable for our actions by making amends to the people we have harmed. We are correcting our wrongs through actions, not just words. We stay close to our sponsor during each amends to stay focused and disciplined.

10. **Perseverance** - We continue and strive to grow in understanding and effectiveness. This takes practice! We have to keep on a steady path. We are walking on the road of happy destiny and to continue this walk takes diligence.

11. **Spiritual Awareness** - We continue to improve our conscious contact with our Higher Power. We practice this through prayer and meditation. We are grateful for all of the blessings we are receiving. We are seeing God's work in all aspects of our lives. We do not question whether God is in control.

12. **Service** - Having experienced a change that keeps us sober one day at a time, we now demonstrate the principles by which we live. We remain in action in our daily life through example. We seek out and are available to help others in need. We continue to carry the message of hope and recovery. We strive to help wherever we can. The hand of AA was there when I needed it! Am I reaching my hand out now?

These are the action principles of the Twelve Steps of Alcoholics Anonymous. They are simply laid out to improve our quality of life. As long as we use these principles each day, we will receive the gift of sobriety.

Honesty

There are signs that humility may be closely related to honesty. This is what AA is talking about when they present the triad of Honesty, Open-mindedness and Willingness as conditions necessary for success in sobriety. If a person practices self-honesty, is open minded about the need for change and is willing to seek improvement, then they certainly have become teachable.

Self-honesty is the main foundation of the AA program. It is the underlying principle in the first step. There are several different levels of honesty, which include cash register honesty, emotional honesty, being honest with others and above all spiritual honesty. All of these levels of honesty are important to us if we want to maintain recovery.

We can learn a great deal about being honest with ourselves from reading Dr. Paul's chapter in the Big Book of Alcoholics Anonymous.... *"Doctor Alcoholic Addict."* This level of honesty has to do with being honest with ourselves and our expectations of people, places and situations.

One of the reasons that we tell lies is, because we are afraid of what we know or what we don't know. We are scared of what others will think of us if maybe we don't know the answer to a question or perhaps if we don't understand something. Or we are fearful of what will be found out about our past. So ultimately, every time we tell a lie, the thing that we fear the most only grows bigger and stronger and pretty soon we have dug ourselves in so deep that we don't know how to get out of any of these situations.

Often at times we are guilty of lying to ourselves. When we do this, it is similar to cheating at solitaire. We don't think it is important because we justify to ourselves that it is not affecting anyone else. The problem with this is, that we continue to maintain a level of dishonesty towards self. How will we be able to improve our character if we insist on lying or cheating, whether it is to ourselves or to others?

If we make mistakes, we have to stop trying to cover them up. We have to stop assigning blame for our own mistakes. We need to start becoming accountable for what we do. If we don't, we get caught up in self-justification, which is a lie in itself. The choice is ours! We can admit our faults and in doing so we start to become a better person. Or we can continue to deny responsibility and end up worse off than what we were yesterday.

Another way we tend to lie to ourselves and to others is by wearing a mask. We pretend to be someone else. This practice probably originates from early childhood. How many of us discovered that when we were young and vulnerable and revealed our true feelings, we were often shamed, ridiculed or scolded? How many times have we heard men say that their fathers told them that real men don't cry or to never show your emotions because it is a sign of weakness? So because of this, we end up becoming dependent on others and are afraid of being abandoned or rejected. Or we shut down altogether and don't let anyone get close enough to us to have any kind of meaningful relationship. We put on a mask to protect ourselves by pretending to be who we are not. As time goes by, the mask becomes so tight that it is almost impossible to remove.

Happiness is a by-product of being true to ourselves. The fact is, most people don't know how to live this way.

They spend a great deal of time and energy trying to please other people just to look good or feel good about themselves. This is called feeding the gorilla. This is just another mask that we put on. Which ever way we look at it, we are only stroking our egos or trying to build some kind of self-worth.

Our true character is often brought to the surface by fear and greed. In times of fear we often face difficulties and disasters. We may have opportunities for financial, career or power. How we approach these extremes when the stakes are high reveals our true selves. The choices we make during these moments of truth exposes the depth of our character.

One way to explore our inner level of honesty and integrity is to look at how much we trust others. We often tend to see the world as we are. If we feel that people are basically dishonest and can't be trusted, this may be revealing more about us than them. One of the problems of lying is not just that people wouldn't believe us, it's also that we can't believe anyone else.

Bill Wilson, one of the co-founders of Alcoholics Anonymous really admired people who would say what was on their minds and speak the truth, just as long as the intent was not to harm anyone. He also knew the perils of rigorous honesty. He fought daily to feed his ego as most of us surely do. So ask yourself! How honest am I with myself and with others? Only you can answer this question truthfully!

Hope

Don't quit before the miracle happens is a term that is heard in AA meetings throughout the world. Whether you are an alcoholic or a family member, we need to remind ourselves that the process of recovery is a combination of action, living one day at a time and having hope for a positive future.

We know that all of this we have mentioned may be the farthest thing from any newcomer's mind. We also know through experience that the despair, loneliness and lack of self-worth that has consumed you will disappear if you stick around long enough and give this way of life a chance.

When going through the trials and tribulations of the recovery process it does take a great deal of strength and courage, not only on the newcomer's part but, also on the ones who are most directly affected. Rather than give in to anger, hopelessness and frustration, getting the support you need will make a difference in the way you deal with the disease of alcoholism.

Having an open mind towards the recovery process is really the key. Many problem drinkers that come to AA don't know what to expect. The majority it seems come for help to control their drinking. They really haven't got a clue about what had caused them to drink in the first place.

It is normal for almost everyone new to the AA program to come in and not want to be noticed. We know this because we have been there. All that we ask is that you come in and look around the rooms at the people who are happy and laughing and caring about others. We ask that you keep an open mind and give it a try.

Hope can never be taken away from you. This is one of the miracles that we are talking about. The reason is that it lives inside of you. It is not something that you can touch and it cannot be taken from you. It is a gift from God, and it doesn't cost anything.

So, when things look bad, as they do many times in our lives , do not give up. As long as you have hope, there is always a chance for a new start.

Hope means to believe in a positive outcome related to events and circumstances in one's life. It is the feeling that what you want to have happen can come true. Hope is not to have to live the way that you have been living anymore. Hope is that force that builds up strength from inside you through guidance from above. It strives to connect reality with a firm belief so that we may accomplish what needs to happen. Hope is the building blocks and the foundation of all human resolve. Our fear only weakens us and try's to destroy this resolve. Hope is therefore definitely more powerful that fear.

Faith

Alcoholics Anonymous, as well as other twelve step fellowships are not religious programs because, all members are entitled to their own personal beliefs. Spirituality within the fellowship is basically defined as behaviors, thoughts and attitudes combined in a consistent manner in which we acknowledge that a power greater than ourselves appears to be at work.

Our Higher Power can be anything to us that is viewed as being something greater than ourselves which ultimately assists us on our journey and helps us to achieve sobriety.

God is mentioned a lot within the program of AA. Having a particular faith or whatever we put our faith into will provide us with the help we need to excel on our path. With a Higher Power in our lives, we acquire peace of mind, endurance, strength and understanding as well as the essential knowledge for us to rise above the problems we encounter in life.

The whole concept of a Higher Power is revealed through the members of AA and all of its literature. Everyone's personal thoughts on a Higher Power will help us in finding our own. On a daily basis we continue to see the miracles that happen in other peoples' lives as a result of their belief in a Higher Power. We begin to want what other people in the program have. We start to learn to be compatible with the concept of having faith and soon begin to find out what our own Higher Power is.

When we hear people talking about God, it is the God of their own understanding. What works for them may not work for us. We will apply our own concept to the God of our own understanding. Faith surrounds the fellowship and we all will eventually adopt our own insight of how we relate to a Higher Power in our lives. Remember that this may take some time to feel comfortable with, especially if you never had believed in God or that you grew up with a God that you did not like.

A Higher Power provides help from either within us or from above us. It doesn't matter where God's guidance comes from. What matters is that we accept the grace when we pray for it. The more our personal relationship grows with our God, the more guidance and strength we will receive.

Although there are some people in the fellowship who choose not to believe in God, the majority does believe. Most of us believe that it is imperative that an alcoholic have faith and trust in God. They agree that it is a cornerstone and that confident faith will ensure better results to staying sober.

The fellowship as a whole is based on an agreement with particular spiritual principles. As we develop spiritually, we will reduce our selfish motives. We will start relying more on help from above that will provide us with truth, knowledge, awareness and success. This spirituality will produce a humility that is the essential component for a successful and fulfilling life of recovery.

This guidance we receive may or may not be noticeable to us at first. We must have faith that our Higher Power is working in our lives and will provide us with the skills we need to improve our character and to be of help to someone else. It is up to us to look for and follow the positive motivations and affirmations that are given to us.

We must always remember that throughout our recovery, no matter what happens, our Higher Power will always love us and will always have the desire to help us walk our path. By knowing this, we can build a loving, faithful and unshakeable relationship with God.

So in order to ensure a lasting recovery, it is necessary to establish a meaningful bond or friendship with God and know that He/She holds all the things we need. It is through this faith that we will attain a true and lasting sober life.

Endless opportunities and chances for our personal spiritual development are made possible by allowing God to guide us on this journey. No longer will we be alone and have to battle life's problems by ourselves. Nor will we need to succumb to our self-inflicted prisons of misery. We will learn to work hand in hand with God to achieve victory from within us. By developing our faith, we will begin to use the one component that keeps us going in life............our hearts.

Courage

When we seek the courage to change the things we can, we are seeking the quality within ourselves through **G**ood **O**rderly **D**irection. If at first we are unable to obtain that quality, then we have other tools available to us that will guide us through the process. Some of these include working with a sponsor, working with others or taking on a commitment. The list is on going. These tools will enable us to deal with the problems of life without the reliance on alcohol.

Accepting the things that we cannot change, which is everything around us, not only calms us, but it brings us to the realization that all events are part of life. When things begin to crumble around us, we will need to maintain focus on our spiritual connection.

Spirituality is defined in a person who has the courage to have faith and believe in the power and presence of God in their lives. Their faith enables them to believe that God is helping them in their times of trouble and pain. Faith is the belief that God will never abandon or forget us during our time of need.

To have any hope or trust in God's mercy, wisdom and justice takes a tremendous amount of courage. This courage enables you to let go and let God guide you. To have the courage to change the things we can, might mean turning over our own apple cart in order that we may do something better and allow a greater light to shine.

Webster's definition of serenity speaks of being free of storms and of unpleasant change. Well guess what! Change is going to come into our lives whether we want it to or not, and not all of it will be pleasant. However, with acceptance and courage we will be able to maintain an inner calm in the face of any and all storms.

Those things we can do nothing about will simply have to be accepted. Those things we can change may not always need to be changed. Deciding not to act on something is often the most courageous of actions that we can take. But, when action is called for, wisdom at the beginning provides the catalyst to make the change for the good for all who are involved.

Courage brings out the possibilities of improving our lives. When we finally take this giant step, we will see how we can diminish frustrations and strive to gain the wisdom that is necessary for unlimited growth. We will get a better understanding of what our purpose in life is.

The courage to believe in ourselves is essential for our ability to accomplish our goals. So maybe we should ask ourselves if it is time to stand up for those things in which we want to achieve.

Courage is not the absence of fear, but the overcoming of it. Fear is a natural part of the disease of alcoholism. Identifying and working through fear is a natural part of recovery. When we no longer are afraid of fear, we begin to recover.

Integrity

When we talk about a person who has integrity, we are saying that they are considered to have a strong moral character. Integrity is thought by many people to be one of the most important virtues a person can possess.

Integrity depends on the consistency of our actions. To achieve integrity, a person must base his or her actions on a well thought out design of moral principles. What they say should be the same as what they do.

Choosing the values that are most important to you and the ones you believe in will define your character. Then live by them visibly every day, at work and at home. Living by your values is one of the most powerful tools available to you to help you be the person you want to be and also how to be the most powerful example to others. It also helps you to accomplish your goals and dreams and to be of service to others.

Honesty is a separate issue that applies to ones personal integrity. To be honest is to apply integrity to a situation or circumstance. Honesty and in integrity always join hand-in-hand without exception. There are very few things that can hurt more than dishonesty. At least being honest will leave a person with some sense of closure and dignity, despite the fact that honesty may sometimes hurt because the truth at times is hard to swallow.

One of the greatest by-products of having integrity is that we gain serenity. As we continue to live a lifestyle of honesty, we will be filled with peace a little more each day. Making honest decisions will get easier and ultimately lead to a better life.

Clearing up the past means that you say what needs to be said. It means to correct any wrongs and make the changes necessary so things will work well. When something comes up, you really need to deal with it immediately.

If you are not satisfied with some area of your life, instead of looking outside for blame or for answers, look within at how you are living. The choices you are making may be out of alignment with what is right for you.

Personal growth requires constant self-examination through self-honesty and the willingness to be humble and to take responsibility for your own life. Knowing yourself and your strengths will give you the perspective you need to learn from your mistakes. When you understand these needs, the potential for growth and service to others we be unlimited.

Willingness

The first three step in recovery are about getting right with God. If we are not convinced or we do not accept these steps, then we will only be doing an injustice to ourselves with the following steps. We have to surrender our entire lives....past, present and future.

Let's take a look at the third step prayer and break it down into sections. *"God I offer myself to You, to build with me and do with me as You will."* (pg. 63 Alcoholics Anonymous) When we offer ourselves to God, we are surrendering to God's guidance in our lives with regard to our actions, thoughts, motives and decisions. We have already admitted to our powerlessness. We also admitted that it's been our selfish motives and brilliant ideas that have gotten us into trouble time after time. So now that we are surrendering ourselves to God so He will lead the way, this shows that we are willing to change the way we do things today. We say we are willing to try something new and are trusting that God knows what to do better than we do.

When we ask God to *"build with me and do with me as Thou will,"* we are humbling ourselves by allowing us to be vulnerable to Him. We are offering ourselves to be available to God and to allow Him to work through us any way He can. We are saying that God has a better plan for me today and I don't want to screw it up by trying to run the show myself. If God has plans for someone else today, and He wants to work through me to bring about those plans, I am willing to cooperate also. God has a purpose for my life. I want to yield to Him so that purpose can be fulfilled. This means that humility is going to have to kick in at some point, right?

Basically the first sentence in the third step prayer lets God know that we are making a conscious decision today to not be in charge. He is the boss and I am not and that is the way I choose to operate today. I believe God doesn't want me to drink alcohol today. Therefore, when I offer myself to God to build with me and do with me as He would today, there's a good chance I won't drink.

The next part of the prayer say's *"Relieve me of the bondage of self, that I may better do Your will."* According to the Big Book Search Engine, the word "self" appears eighty-nine times in its text. The word "selfish" appears sixteen times and is combined with other unpleasant descriptive words such as; selfish and foolish, selfish and dishonest, selfish and frightened and selfish and inconsiderate.

On page 71, the Big Book tells us that self-will has blocked us off from God. Page 124 teaches us that our self-centered views are in direct conflict with our new way of living. When we look at page 116, it tells us that people who are self-centered are afflicted with pride, self-pity, vanity, selfishness and dishonesty. We are challenged in our fourth steps to see where we have been selfish, dishonest, self-seeking and frightened.

Time and time again throughout AA's literature, we are warned that self-knowledge, self-reliance and self-confidence cannot be trusted and generally will amount to nothing more than self-delusion. We have found that booze isn't the problem. Self is the problem! The theme of the Big Book is the process we take by which God is able to rid us of the bondage of self. It explains this in detail on page 62.

There should be nothing more important in our recovery than our quest to be set free from the bondage of self. We who have been through the steps are convinced that this is not something we can accomplish on our own. This is why it is so important to have a sponsor that has gone through the steps themselves the way they are suggested. It may be the most difficult thing we will ever do. But we are certain that with all of the progress we make in this area, our lives will get better. Not only will we benefit, but so will others with whom we come in contact with. As long as we let self run the show, God is not in charge. If this is the case, we are not able to be of any service to anyone else.

There are a few questions that we need to ask ourselves. First! Do we even want to change? Are we truly sick and tired of being sick and tired? Do we understand, at least to some degree that we have brought many of our own problems on ourselves and that unless something changes in our thinking, our attitudes and our behaviors, then nothing much will change with regard to our alcoholism.

Some people get uncomfortable and fearful when their lives start going too smoothly. Fear can keep us stuck! A lot of people say, "*I know I'm powerless over alcohol and my life is unmanageable. I might be able to accept the fact that there is a Power greater than me that can restore me to sanity.*" But that is as far as they take it. Some cry out, "*recovery will not be forced on me!*" Step Three is where we say, "*I AM READY TO GET WELL!*"

*The request in the third step prayer, "**Take away my difficulties**"* causes us to ask ourselves a few important questions also. Do we want our difficulties taken away? Or will we justify that they might not be all that bad and just maybe take some of them away? Is whatever God we are praying to able to take away these difficulties? (This is where the door-knob theory fails.) Door-knobs can't take away anything! Door-knobs do not have any power!

Finally, are we willing to risk living without these difficulties?

"That victory over them may bear witness to those I would help of Thy power, Thy love and Thy way of life."

We don't ask God to relieve our difficulties so that we can just go on our way and live selfishly and self-centeredly as we have always done in the past, only looking out for our own wants and needs. If nothing changes in our character, then we are still the same person. God knows not to leave us stuck in our selfish egos. He knows where that will lead us. But He also knows that sometimes we don't have enough sense to figure this out for ourselves. This is why our dependency on God needs to strengthen.

We are specifically stating here in this phase that we would like our difficulties to be taken out of the way so that others can witness with their own eyes what God has done for us. This is what's known as a greater purpose. A bigger picture! God's work in my life is not all about me! (Imagine that!)

The entire program of recovery is spelled out in the Big Book and the Twelve and Twelve. Both of these books along with other approved literature keeps us focused away from our own selfish, self-centered desires and helps teach us the vital principle of "the constant thought of helping others." Healing takes place not only when we try harder, but when we let go and let God work through us to be of service to someone else. By helping others heal, we get to heal. By helping others grow spiritually, we get to grow spiritually.

When we are being of service to someone else, we benefit because we get out of our own self-centeredness. Helping someone else isn't that difficult. Start by opening

25

the door for someone. Bring someone a cup of coffee. Ask someone to sit with you at a meeting. Give someone a ride if they don't have a vehicle. Pick up the neighbor's trash cans. Let someone tell you about their day and really listen to them. It doesn't have to be complicated.

Surrendering to this way of life is so much easier to talk about than it is to put into action. We might find the idea of thinking of others before we think of ourselves almost impossible. Trusting God to take care of our needs is a very scary thing at first. You would think that simply relaxing that white-knuckled grip and allowing control to slip from your fingers would be a pretty easy thing to do. We have discovered it's totally against human nature. Why? Because we want what we want, and we want it when we want it, and it is usually NOW!

By nature we will put our own needs above the needs of anyone else on earth. We want to be the captain of our own ship, the director in our own play or the leader of our own band. By nature we don't want anyone telling us what to do! "If this is the case for you, then tell me..... how's that been working for you so far?

Getting drunk seemed to be the only thing we could ever accomplish with any regularity. So, let's re-focus our attention on the phrase once again; ***"...that victory over them may bear witness to those I would help of Your power, Your love, and Your way of life."*** When we read this, three questions come to mind. Does the Higher Power we are praying to indeed have power? Is the Higher Power we are praying to capable of feeling and expressing love? What is our Higher Power's way of life?

The word "victory" is such a permanent word. Is there any such thing as temporary victory? Either you WIN or you LOSE. Either you're a victor or you're not. Do we pray for total victory or only partial victory?

"May I do Thy will always" Does this part remind us of the foxhole prayers we used to say when we needed to get out of a jam? When we let self dig us in so deep that we didn't know how to get out! Then and only then did we ask God to guide us? So if we ask Him for the guidance in doing His will always, are we going to ask for it every day, or only when we think we need it? Are we ready and willing to make a commitment to God every day? Or will we continue to let that door slam shut?

Humility

Humility is described as a state of being humble without pride and yet still being teachable. A person who is humble is thought to be modest and does not think that he or she is better or more important than others.

Let's not confuse humility with being humiliated. Humiliation is considered to be the act of lowering someone else's esteem only to build ourselves up, where as, humility is to be free of pride through the gains of self-respect.

It is probably safe to say that most of us who have been able to maintain any amount of sobriety have acquired some degree of humility. For instance, if we have realized that our past drinking behavior was full of humiliation toward others and we acknowledge this to be unacceptable behavior and we want to change, then we have received a measure of humility.

Bill Wilson (co-founder of AA) talked about humility often. He admitting to battling with his pride when he was drinking and also well into his sobriety. He knew that he would not be able to get or maintain any emotional sobriety without having pride removed. He also knew that the only way to do this was to first admit that he was powerless over his pride. Once he did this, he could then apply the other steps.

Our search for humility, if we are really serious about our sobriety, truly is a daily task. Step Ten tells us we need to take a personal inventory. When we look for the necessary conditions for success, we have to look at how the program will help change our entire intake and outlook on life. A few things to look at that might help us gain humility are self-honesty, willingness and being open minded enough to be teachable in these areas.

A person who practices rigorous honesty usually has a pretty good understanding of themselves. This will lead towards good self-esteem, which in turn helps to keep them from feeling victimized by pride.

Time after time, many of us battle over the need to be honest and the fear that we may have to admit we are wrong. In which the outcome is that we may look bad to others. God forbid that we surrender our fears to gain a little humility.

When we take a step back and look at all of the facts of any situation without reacting on instant emotion, we are able to see what is true and what is not. This allows us to form an honest approach to the situation in realizing that, first, we are powerless over not only by what just occurred, but by what the outcome will also be. Second, we were willing enough to have an open mind to be teachable and to learn how to deal with the problem in a more acceptable way without having a need for praise or reassurance to feed our egos.

Human nature pushes us to learn to be a better person if we are sober. It wants us to be more humble and to try to be more honest. Humility, whether you call it being self-honest or teachable is what we have been looking for our whole lives. Unless we are vigilant in practicing this way of life, then pride will always be the victor over us and divert us from doing the right thing.

We must apply these principles along with the other tools we have been given on a daily basis in order to maintain and improve our sobriety. If we choose not to do this, then we have missed the true meaning of sobriety altogether.

Forgiveness

There are definitely times when someone does something to us in a negative way and through no fault of our own we end up with resentment. When this happens, if we are not spiritually fit, we will try to justify this resentment. There is no place for a justified resentment in an alcoholic's life. It will consume us just as much as an unjustified resentment will.

Anger is poison whether we think it is justified or not. If we think we have become a victim, then we need to pray for this person. Forgiveness allows us to move on with our lives and grants us the freedom we have always been searching for.

Resentments usually are feelings that have been built on assumption or expectation, i.e.; *"When you didn't invite me to the party, I assumed you didn't like me anymore."* or *"I expected that since we were seeing each other, that you would want me to meet your friends."* If these feelings aren't dealt with immediately they will fester into an infection. One of the easiest ways to deal with this is to ask God to help this person. We ask Him for guidance and patience to keep us from getting angry. We have to realize that this person may not be emotionally stable as well.

"If you have a resentment you want to be free of, if you will pray for that person or thing that you resent you will be free. If you will ask in your prayer for everything you want for yourself to be given to them, you will be free. Ask for their health, their prosperity, their happiness and you will be free. Even when you don't really want it for them and your prayers are only words and

you don't mean it, go ahead and do it anyway. Do it everyday for two weeks and you will find you have come to mean it and want it for them and you will realize that where you feel bitterness and resentment and hatred, you now feel compassionate understanding and love." (Alcoholics Anonymous pg. 552-4ᵗʰ edition)

We can't just say these words without meaning. We have to have faith in the process. We have to believe that as a result of the process of praying for forgiveness, that this will set us free. Pg. 66 in the Big Book tells us that; **"It is plain that a life which includes deep resentment leads only to futility and unhappiness."**

Resentments are like drinking poison and waiting for the other person to die. If we can't practice forgiveness, we are only hurting ourselves by our own actions. Take a hurt that was left over from something that happened back in high school. Over the years we added to this resentment. We rehearsed and replayed the hurt. We blamed them for our hurt feelings so much, that this toxic resentment took on a life of its own. It's not very likely that the person who we even blamed for our hurt feelings even remembers us. We are the one that is mad. So who gets hurt by this resentment? Hanging on to old resentments will only keep us anchored in the past and not allow us to move forward in recovery.

Forgiveness is the first step to freedom from any of our resentments. If we keep hanging on to any resentment, we will be consumed with self-pity, hate or blame. We have to drop the rock in order to recover. The price is too high to pay for us not to forgive.

This doesn't mean that we have to become a martyr for someone else to walk on us. We don't have to accept something that is just plain unacceptable. So, if you are having a hard time with forgiveness maybe you should ask yourself what the payoff is? There must be a reason that you are refusing to let go.

Resentments are a huge part of our alcoholic lives. The Twelve Steps help to keep us aware of them continuously, whether they are glaring at us or if they are in hiding. Steps eight and nine offer us an opportunity to make amends to those we have resented in the past. Step ten gives us the opportunity to reflect daily on any resentments that may arise. It also lets us get rid of any unwanted garbage that will cause us to stay in self or worse yet to take a drink.

Forgiveness is a gift that you allow yourself to have. It releases us from the burden of anger and pain. When we choose to forgive, whether it is to ourselves or to someone else, we choose to live in today and tomorrow instead of the past. This does not mean we have to forget, but it does mean we need to release and go on. Forgiveness doesn't happen on it's own and it doesn't happen overnight. It takes prayer and practice.

There are certain things that we must remember. We need to forgive ourselves for thinking that we are not worthy of love, happiness and joy. We need to stop judging ourselves. Find the strength and courage that will allow yourself to be vulnerable to change. Start making better choices in your life that are spiritually rewarding. Live for today and begin to enjoy the journey that life is presenting to you.

Discipline

Alcoholism is an incurable disease. Reprieve from the disease and recovery from the devastation caused by it is what every alcoholic strives for. Without having a strict adherence to the principles of AA, one of which is daily discipline, the alcoholic is likely to relapse.

The alcoholic must follow this program of simplicity in order to obtain any quality sobriety. It will require diligence and patience not only from the alcoholic, but also from family and friends. When the alcoholic was out there drinking, alcohol made all of the decisions. Their actions and behaviors most likely didn't go unnoticed by any of their peers. Their actions may not have always been physical towards others. But they certainly were mentally, emotionally and spiritually misaligned.

If the alcoholic is to maintain sobriety, then attendance at AA meetings is imperative. In the beginning attending meetings must be daily. Taking direction from a sponsor is vital. They will help guide you to make the right decisions. After you get some time in the program you will start to find a balance in both your home life and going to meetings. Remember that it may have taken years of alcoholic drinking and thinking to get to this point. Recovery won't happen overnight. This is where not only discipline comes into play, but patience also.

At times it may seem that the only one benefiting from sobriety is the alcoholic. The family may start to feel neglected. Friends may be put on hold and household responsibilities may be put on the back burner. Our friends and loved one's may think that this is not much different from active alcoholism. The truth is that they are not used to us trying to do the right things in life.

They aren't used to us being dependable and responsible. So this is where we need to sit down and explain as calmly as possible, that right now we have to take care of ourselves. Because if we don't then we will end up right back where we were before. Let them know that the balance of meetings and home life will happen soon. Let them know that you want to be there when the miracles start to happen in your life and theirs.

Again, try to remember that alcoholism is a deadly and incurable disease that effects the body, mind and spirit. It is not something that you caught a month or a year ago. The progression of the disease started many years before. It worsened over time until the alcohol nearly destroyed the alcoholic and all who were around them. Arresting the disease and recovering from it will take the rest of your life one day at a time.

Perseverance

During early stages of recovery it is very difficult to avoid giving in to the craving for alcohol. This is why we must persevere. It is critical to focus on sobriety for that day. The need may be to break it down to hour by hour or even the next few minutes if that will help you from taking that first drink.

As hard as you may try, there is little else that you may think about in the early days of not drinking. The situation with alcohol will always be on your mind and probably should be in this period of getting sober. Eventually in time when the withdrawals stop and your mind begins to clear a little you will get on with your life. You will start to regain a somewhat normal lifestyle.

Practicing perseverance early in sobriety can only be a benefit in the long run. The longer we stay sober, the more we are challenged to change. Sometimes the change happens whether we want it to or not. As the days turn into months and then into years, we will eventually welcome these changes in our lives. We will begin to adapt to our new sobriety. We will find out it helps if we have had a spiritual awakening along the way, or at least a clear understanding of a Higher Power.

When a recovering alcoholic finally "Gets It." Everything starts to make sense and your future doesn't seem nearly as difficult to comprehend as it once did. This is a time to remain vigilant and yet be optimistic. Good things will start to happen if only given a chance.

To others you may always be labeled as an alcoholic or the one with a drinking problem. This is not who you are though, in spite of what path alcohol has led you down. You are the one who is successfully waging a battle against the disease of alcoholism through daily perseverance. In the beginning you may have been forged into the fire of emotional torment. But by persevering you emerged a stronger, more confident person. Let this be who others see when they start to judge you. More importantly let this be how you see yourself.

Every day we live this sober life, it is so important that we renew our dedication to this program which gave us our freedom and our life. A new freedom and a spiritual way of life. That was the solution for which there was no concept until we came through the doors of AA. So how important is it to us to rededicate ourselves to a primary purpose, to stay sober and to try to help another alcoholic, each day. Failure to do this will lead back to the insanity and chaos we came from. Unless you want to go there again, it's up to you to come up with the willingness and perseverance to continue to do what the old timers so freely gave to us.

Spiritual Awareness

The gift of sobriety is given to us as a daily reprieve based on the continued maintenance of our spiritual condition. When we start to think that we can stop working towards an in-depth program of spiritual maintenance, or that we can just simply ask our Higher Power for guidance and thank Him at night. Then this is the day we start heading down a path towards a relapse.

Recovering from alcoholism is not a self-help program designed for the purpose of gaining knowledge, strength and willpower so we can beat this disease. Recovery is about recognizing, that by ourselves we are powerless to solve the problem. In order to receive the gift of sobriety and start the recovery process, we must first admit we need God's help. The EGO must be smashed!

Anyone that has gone thru the steps will tell you that the problem is spiritual and so is the solution. This is why sobriety really depends totally on looking after our spiritual health.

Countless people have struggled to stay sober with just their own willpower. Some, but very few fight the process until grace comes. Many will continue to relapse over and over again. Some of us will just give up and never make it back. So in order to stay sober we must find a way to get connected and stay connected to God and others around us that are striving for the same spiritual way of life. Because if we don't we will slip back into the illusion of self-control.

If we take the time to look around the rooms of AA, we will see many people and not only the newcomers leading their lives in quiet desperation. They appear to be in constant frustration of trying to fill their spiritual void.

They cover up their pain with distractions and excuses. They don't even realize they are starving themselves into a dark abyss of loneliness. Alcoholics are physically predisposed to escape themselves in ways that will go directly into a downward spiral of self-destruction.

"Reminding ourselves that we have decided to go to any lengths to find a spiritual experience, we ask that we be given strength and direction to do the right thing, no matter what the personal consequences may be." Alcoholics Anonymous, 4th edition, Into Action, pg. 79

"Acceptance is the answer to all my problems today" is the opening line of one of the most popular passages in recovery literature. To simply accept that things are the way they are, seems like the ultimate challenge. Could they be changed? They probably could be! Is it possible that they could be improved? Maybe! But right at this moment, things are the way they are and to be able to find any acceptance of this is a tremendous freedom and relief.

"It is a spiritual axiom that every time we are disturbed, no matter what the cause, there is something wrong with us", Bill Wilson wrote this on page 92 of the Twelve Steps and Twelve Traditions. You might be asking what exactly does axiom mean? One definition is that, "it is a self evident principle or one that is accepted as true without proof as basis for argument."

When we end up giving people, places or things control over our lives and the situation does not turn out to our satisfaction, we may say that they make us angry or afraid. The truth is that we may say or do something that helps to create these same conflicts in our lives. Step Ten suggests that we take responsibility for this fact, clean up our role in these matters and practice forgiveness. If we show courtesy towards others and are as kind and loving as possible, then we are treating them like we would want to be treated. Do you believe this treatment towards others is reasonable? If you don't, then you have missed a major part of the solution to your problems.

AA literature is very clear on the recovery process. It tells us exactly how to solve not only our drinking problem, but also our living problem. It is explained very clearly in Chapter Two of the Big Book; There Is A Solution. The total design for living is laid out in the first one hundred and sixty four pages.

The founders of AA tell us, in order to remove defects of character, a person must engage in a spiritual path and seek a spiritual solution. Spiritual solutions are as old as man and are as universal throughout most religions. These solutions have been taught by every spiritual leader for thousands of years. This solution teaches us to become free from the bondage of self.

What is bondage of self? It is the flaws of our self that the alcoholic has built through the process of his or her life. When self becomes chronic, or in other words, their drinking has lead to physical and psychological harm to themselves or to others which has drastically impaired their social abilities, the alcoholic has to create a character to protect them and defend them at all costs. Because we have no spiritual fitness in our lives we have no idea that the self and character that we built are false.

Every true spiritual path offers a way, a method and a program to return to living life on life's terms and to live sober. In sobriety, life is experienced just as it is. When the false self no longer rules a person, its demand for power, money, status, reputation, excess, drama, etc., no longer rule that person's thoughts or actions. As a result, the person becomes free of that bondage. The person is free to enjoy simplicity. Through this recognition, a person can find joy, pleasure, contentment and fulfillment. They realize that they have been restored to sanity. They again can embrace life with a child-like innocence. Not because everything is perfect, but because it is all part of life and life is good enough on life's own terms. This is what the promises in the Big Book offer us.

The principle inside Step Eleven teaches us about the awareness of God. This step reminds us that we have a God that we understand. It also tells us that now would be a good idea to pray and meditate and keep God in our hearts.

The hard part of this step if there is one, is to learn how to pray and meditate not only with the awareness of God, but also that we know what His will for us is. The Twelve & Twelve reminds us that although it is a beautiful thing to pray for someone else, it is not up to us to think we know what God's will is for them.

Let's not forget meditation. Most of us make too much of the how to meditate. The Twelve & Twelve gives us a perfect example of simple meditation using the prayer of St. Francis of Assisi. Try reading this prayer over and over again and then just sit quietly and think about what it means. Listening for the answer to your prayers takes more than a couple of minutes. So don't be in such a hurry. This is a simple way to meditate, but who say's meditation has to be difficult? For most of us, this will be about as much meditation as we can really handle.

Service

When we say to be of service to others, we don't mean doing a deed in return for something. We are talking about being kind, unselfish and generous without any expectations. In this regard, no positive act is insignificant and no person in need of assistance is too low on the scale of life for your time and attention.

Unselfish service is marked by humility. This is a trait that is hard to find in this age of egoism. More often than not, many of us are guilty of the latter.

Literature in AA consistently stresses the importance of helping others to get sober. Being of service to others is plainly addressed in the Twelfth Step. It tells us that by; *"Having had a spiritual awakening as the result of these steps, we tried to carry this message to alcoholics and to practice these principles in all our affairs."* **Alcoholics Anonymous**

This step really encourages members to give back to the program that saved their life by helping others to achieve sobriety. Doing twelve step work is broadly defined and may include being anything that may help others. This may include setting up chairs or cleaning coffee cups after the meetings. These commitments are great for newcomers in helping them to get to know others in recovery. Eventually they will get more involved in how the meetings are maintained. They will understand how the general service representative and other offices function.

One of the most common service commitments in AA is the role of sponsorship. This is a core part of twelve step work that involves helping the newcomer get adjusted to this way of life. Sponsors tend to serve as role models if you will, for the new members. They offer their guidance in working the twelve steps of the program. Sponsors are used as sounding boards for listening to the people they sponsor. When they share their own experiences, it is much easier for the newcomer to start to identify. A sponsor should be someone who has gone through the twelve steps with their sponsors. Preferably they should be of the same gender, only to avoid any extra curricular activity.

There are pamphlets on sponsors in pretty much every meeting, along with other topics that will help you in recovery. Each member of Alcoholics Anonymous is a potential sponsor of any new member and should clearly recognize the obligations and duties of such a responsibility.

AA defines a sponsorship in this way: **"An alcoholic who has made some progress in the recovery program who shares that experience on a continuous, individual basis with another who is attempting to attain or maintain sobriety through AA" Every sponsor is different, just as each sponsee is different, but certain activities, responsibilities, and obligations are common in all sponsor/sponsee relationships. They are all working to help one another remain sober for just one more day by sharing themselves with one another.**

To be of service to others does not need to end with helping only people in AA. The more we help others, no matter where we are or what we are involved in will only bring us happiness and secure our sobriety.

Relapse

We hear people giving these excuses all the time; *"I've been to AA before and it didn't work for me. I went for a week or two, or a month or a year and then I started slacking off meetings."* Usually when this begins to happen it's because they either didn't really work the steps or they did and they started feeling better and thought they didn't need to go any more. Many of us start feeling really good and wonder, why? The reason is AA is starting to work and unfortunately instead of us wanting more of it, we think we have a handle on our drinking. We begin to believe the lies in our heads that tells us we don't have to go to as many meetings. So the cycle begins and we start doing other stuff because we feel good.

This is one of the greatest lies of alcoholism. It deceives the alcoholic. It fools the family and they start coming up with seemingly justifiable reasons to go to fewer meetings such as; *"I'm working more and can't find the time." I'm giving you money, where before I was drinking it all away."* Instead of going to an AA meeting they will go to church. Not that church is a bad thing, but try telling the person sitting next to you about some of the things you did while you were drinking and that you feel like getting drunk. They will probably move to another seat. Or maybe instead of going to a meeting, they take their kids to a movie. Before you know it they are attending fewer and fewer meetings and they stop going all together.

We may hear them say that the meetings are boring. Or they resent this or that about their home group. They think the rooms are too dark and dingy. Maybe the seats are to uncomfortable. It was raining. That guy always dominates the meeting when he speaks. That person is arrogant. Whatever the excuse, any excuse will do!

The problem with that is they get to a point where they think they can get sober themselves. Then something triggers and the stress hits. Whatever the stress of life is at the time. And instead of going to a meeting to share what's going on and getting all the support and feedback they need, they turn again to the drink.

Why do we have to go to so many meetings? Many who are coming back or who are new to AA go to ninety meetings in ninety days. This gets them back to basics and builds a foundation of security. When those ninety are done, then they go to another ninety. Usually it's a good idea to go to a minimum of at least five meetings a week for your first year. People who seem to stay sober usually go to seven to ten meetings a week in the first year. It's like taking out more insurance in a policy.

The newcomer may often say; *"All I do is go to work and go to meetings."* We may tell them; *"Well that's all you should be doing in your first year of sobriety. Because anything more than that, you're probably doing too many things. You have to stay focused. It's a serious disease."*

What about the relapse in early sobriety? There are many withdrawal times that the body goes through. Some are at thirty days and may go all the way into eighteen months or longer. These periods for most people are bad withdrawal times, not only from the booze, but from the inability to live life without alcohol. That means at those times stress really hits and if they haven't been going to regular meetings the stress really increases at that time. There is more of a chance of drinking again. If people are going to regular meetings, they just know to double up on their meetings at that time. Go to two a day or three a day. Talk with somebody afterwards. Call your sponsor. Get to the meeting early and talk to people. Those withdrawal times will pass. But they will need extra meetings and extra help at that time.

We can't stress enough that a relapse for the alcoholic is a life and death situation. Any relapse means that you are gambling with your life. One or two drinks will inevitably lead back to excessive drinking within a short period. This has been shown to be a fact time and time again. People who relapse often die from accidents such as overdose, suicide or medical problems. If you have a damaged liver and begin drinking again, your liver will immediately return to its most damaged state.

Some people are fortunate to halt the relapse before achieving a lasting life of sobriety. A small minority though, manage to have none at all. The best policy is to learn from those who have never relapsed as well as those who have. Find out how each guarded against it and tried to avoid it. Of course not relapsing at all is the best scenario for all of us.

While accepting the reality of its potential, we should not use the fact that it could happen as an excuse for actually having a relapse or not trying desperately to avoid one. The first relapse or the next one may be your last!

Once we have detoxed our bodies and begun to get sober, the key issue in our minds is to stay sober. In order to do this and by using the "ONE DAY AT A TIME" tool, we will need to understand and accept that we are alcoholic. We also need to realize that all the years of being alcohol dependent have programmed our bodies and minds to react instinctively to emotions, feelings and situations.

Many people who relapse say that when they took that first drink, it seemed like they were stuck on auto pilot. There is a truth in this! We have trained ourselves often for years and even decades to automatically reach for the drink as the means of finding pleasure, relief or escape from the troubles of everyday life. We truly did not know there was an alternative. Non-alcoholic people will find other ways of dealing with these issues, but we only know the drink. When we relapse we run the alcoholic insanity film over again in our minds. We play out our part and once the act is done, reality will set in and we wake up to have to face the painful consequences of our destructive behavior.

In order to remain sober we have to de-program ourselves so that we automatically recoil from the temptation and do not take that first drink. To do this we have to first pinpoint the dangerous triggers which can provoke these temptations to drink in order to immediately avoid them at any cost. Then gradually we have to learn new strategies and methods to deal with everyday life on a sober basis.

We can classify these into three main areas, starting with internal feelings and emotions which overwhelm us and can lead us to back to drinking. These might be negative emotions or feelings like anger, sadness, grief, jealousy, loneliness, hate, boredom and depression from which we search for relief through alcohol. On the other hand they can also be good feelings such as euphoria, happiness, exaggerated self-confidence or any other number of feelings that seem positive in our lives. These all are linked to celebration and reward. These can equally lead us to drinking without thinking. Be aware of both negative and positive feelings, because they both can be dangerous to our sobriety if left untreated.

We realize that it is not easy to avoid our emotions and feelings. One can not just stop depression or simply avoid anger and feelings of sadness. This is part of our make-up to be able to express. It is how we express and react to these feelings that is the key. Therefore , we will need to explore what are the most dangerous emotions which we associate with drinking. Then we need to realize that these are separate issues from drinking and are part of the human condition. Having recognized these emotions as separate issues from our *Sobriety Priority,* we need to find ways on how to deal and express these emotions.

Next we need to look at external situations, places and people which can trigger not only our drinking but our attitude. Certain situations, places and social relationships in which we habitually drank may have been bars, parties, dinners, after work socializing, sporting events, isolation at home, concerts, holidays, birthdays etc. It can even be the company of certain people like old drinking buddies, colleagues, a business partner or just being in front of the TV at home alone. Certain music, smells, and foods can also be triggers associated with drinking. These situations are associated with strong emotions of pleasure and escape. Memories have been established in our brain which automatically flips a switch when we find ourselves in such circumstances and trigger the behavioral response of drinking. It might happen consciously or it may come from deep down in the subconscious only to sneak up on us unexpectedly. Often by then it is too late. Remember that it is cunning, baffling and powerful and to say the least very patient.

Unhealthy patterns of behavior and habits when we first get sober will often make us feel like fish out of water. We don't know what to do with our time. If we don't begin to plan and structure a new way of life, then we are at risk of falling back into old patterns and routines such as any of the ones we mentioned before. Initially we may not drink while doing these things. We may drink a coke or have a cup of coffee to show ourselves or others that we are fine. Nevertheless we are acting the role of a dry drunk where the drink has been temporarily displaced.

Of course it is not always possible to avoid places where alcohol is being served. Staying sober is a great personal achievement and one can not and should not cut oneself off from life and live like a hermit. The difference however, is the degree to which we put ourselves in these places, situations and gatherings for which we previously drank. We have to make very certain what our motives are for going to such places. We also need to have an escape plan in case things start to get uncomfortable.

We may not realize it, but by being in these situations we are feeding our thoughts, feelings and emotions which we had when we were drinking. By encouraging the growth of such alcoholic behaviors and thoughts, we are then only one step away from the act of drinking. When we fall back into old habits and patterns we are only rehearsing our role.

Whether we are alcoholic or not, people are creatures of habit who tend to fall back into old routines, especially in times of difficulty or stress. Our tendency to do these is therefore stronger than the average person. If one keeps moving in these circles of addictive behaviors, it will only be a matter of time before they go out again. As they say; *"If you hang out in a barber shop long enough, you will eventually get a hair cut."*

It really is essential to break away from old habits and behaviors as fast as possible. We need to spend as much time as possible in meetings and talking with others. This is because we don't often notice what is happening with us. We aren't able to recognize all the warning signs that our body is telling us. Others might be able to see them and warn us.

Make a list of places, people and situations to avoid and prepare an excuse for not going. Talk these things over with your sponsor and with people in your home group. Don't give in to pressure from others to be somewhere you shouldn't be. If you can't speak the truth, then say you are ill, because you really are. You are recovering from a life threatening illness! Your life comes first! Your priority is your sobriety. Draw out a day plan hour by hour. Think of all new, safe places and people to hang around with and do things you like. Sobriety is not a death sentence! Reward yourself with fun for having saved your own life.

Building a new life is not an easy thing to do. We will have to deal with the wreckage of our past and we will suffer mood swings along with some ups and downs throughout the course of sobriety. On the other hand we don't have to do this alone. By following a few simple suggestions from the program, a sober and rewarding life will gradually emerge. This doesn't mean it will be without problems and tragedies along the way. That's just life!

We will learn how to deal with our emotions without reaching for the bottle. Our self-confidence will grow and our trust in God will strengthen. We will be able to deal with the world on His terms and not the terms of alcohol. We will learn to establish healthier patterns of behavior based on our new life style. Life will become richer and more worth living. We will grow and develop ourselves and feel that we fit in with society. We will realize that we have a purpose in life.

Depression in Sobriety

One of the things that many alcoholics suffer from after they stop drinking is depression. They may find that after they have done a complete inventory, they were depressed even before they drank. Their depression can be so debilitating at times it may feel as if they have reached the end of life and can't find their way back. Periods of confusion become more frequent, last longer and cause more problems.

The alcoholic often feels angry with themselves because of the inability to figure simple things out. Relationships become strained with friends, family and AA members. They often feel threatened when people talk about the changes in their behavior and mood swings. The conflicts continue to increase in spite of efforts to resolve them. They begin to feel guilty and remorseful about their role in their relations with others.

Bill Wilson suffered severely from depression even well after he got sober. Other members of AA and people close to him often accused him of not working the program. We all know that if it wasn't for the founders of AA, the majority of us wouldn't have been able to get sober and live as productive members of society. We also need to acknowledge the fact that our founders went through the same dilemmas as we do today and that depression is one of them. Depression functions much like an addiction. Many of us can attest that it too is an illness and that it needs its own recovery process.

The alcoholic will often try to act as if he or she doesn't care about the problems that are occurring. This is only to hide the feelings of helplessness and a growing lack of self-respect and self-confidence. By this time fear has already taken over. They will isolate themselves from people who can help. They do this by throwing fits of anger that drive others away. Or they may criticize and put others down by quietly withdrawing from others.

Things may seem so bad that they begin to think that they might as well drink because things couldn't get any worse. This is when denial is at its peak and they start to realize how severe their problems are. They see how unmanageable their life has become and how little power or control they have to solve any of their problems. This awareness is extremely painful and very frightening.

When the alcoholic experiences these episodes of anger, frustration, resentment and irritability, they tend to over-react to day-to-day things. Stress and anxiety will increase because they fear they may resort to violence. The efforts to control themselves just add to the stress and tension of any situation. They may become so depressed that they start to have difficulty accomplishing normal routines like minor household chores and even personal hygiene. At times there may be thoughts of suicide that could be induced by drinking or drug use as a way to end the insanity. It becomes so severe and persistent that it cannot be ignored or hidden from others.

Difficulty sleeping and restlessness are often marked by strange and frightening dreams. Because of exhaustion they may sleep for twelve to twenty hours at a time. These sleeping marathons may happen frequently. They may stop getting up or going to bed at any regular times. Sometimes they are unable to sleep at all and end this results in over sleeping at other times.

It becomes more difficult to keep appointments and to attend social events. They feel rushed and overburdened at times and then have nothing to do at other times. They are unable to follow through on plans and decisions. They begin to experience tension, frustration, fear or anxiety that keeps them from doing what really needs to be done.

Some bouts of depression seem to be most severe during unplanned or unstructured events. Fatigue, loss of appetite and loneliness make the depression worse. They end up separating themselves from other people. Getting angry and irritable with other people tends to increase. Often they complain that nobody cares or understands what they are going through.

In a letter that Bill Wilson wrote, he says; I keep asking myself, *"Why can't the Twelve Steps work to release depression?"* By the hour, I stared at the St. Francis prayer.... *" It is better to comfort than to be comforted."* Here was the formula all right, but why didn't it work? Suddenly I realized what the matter was... My basic flaw had always been dependence, almost absolute dependence on people or circumstances to supply me with prestige, security and the like. Failing to get these things according to my perfectionist dreams and specifications, I had fought for them. And when defeat came, so did my depression.

Reinforced by what grace I could find in prayer, I had to exert every ounce of will and action to cut off these faulty emotional dependences upon people and upon circumstances. Then only could I be free to love as Francis had loved. ***Grapevine, January 1958***

So when the alcoholic stops attending meetings, stops calling others and stops living the steps. They will start to find excuses to justify these life saving tools and fail to recognize all of their benefits. They may develop an attitude that says; *"These meetings and steps aren't making me feel better, so why should I make them a priority?"* When in fact, if they were attending meetings on a regular basis, working the steps and trying to comfort others, they wouldn't be able to focus their negative thoughts on themselves and their personal desires and egos would begin to deflate.

History, especially when we look back at Bill Wilson, shows us that it is neither helpful nor useful to look at a person's depression as a moral failure or lack of willpower. It simply is a physical allergy combined with mental obsession.

Bill didn't just stop with AA. He would eventually get into therapy, which some of us may have to do. He also corresponded briefly with Carl Jung. Bill wrote Jung to thank him for steering a friend of his toward a spiritual solution for his drinking problem. That in fact led Bill to his own spiritual experience. Jung wrote back confirming his belief that addiction is a "spiritual thirst for wholeness."

All of us, if we truly want to be free of self, need to find a balance in our physical, mental, spiritual and emotional ways. We must realize that stopping drinking is just the beginning for us. The bigger picture is to find out who we had become as a result of our drinking, how we acted and reacted to others emotionally and how we can improve ourselves daily as the result of working the Twelve Steps of Alcoholics Anonymous in all areas of our lives.

Self-pity

Alcoholics are definitely known for being stubborn. Most of us didn't even know what the word humble meant when we came through the doors of AA. There isn't a blue print that defines all alcoholics, but we do share many qualities and most of those are nothing to brag about.

It seems though, that the most common character defect of an alcoholic is their selfishness. It is like having a total disregard for others. Alcoholics, when they are drinking don't care for anyone or anything except for where their next drink is coming from. They will sacrifice everything to be able to fall into the arms of intoxication. They literally end up destroying relationships and families. Financial ruin, damaged health, lost careers and a future all get put on a back burner.

Being selfish in recovery can actually be a benefit. Especially in the beginning when its purpose is to keep focused on staying sober. After all, we hear it said in the rooms all the time that this is a selfish program.

In the early stages of recovery we must make every effort not only to recognize our self-centered ways when we were out there drinking. But also to see how it is affecting us in our new found sobriety. Specifically we need to be aware of the kind of behavior that makes us angry when things aren't going our way.

Self-pity is an extreme form of immaturity. Nobody ever holds a gun to your head and forces you to drink and tells you not to stop. Self-pity in recovery is common among all of us, but left untreated it is very destructive and serves no purpose at all. It shows a major lack of confidence and an inability to deal with adversity.

A newcomer can get so wrapped up in self-pity that they will try to convince others that they are somehow a victim of circumstances created by someone else. They believe they are justified in feeling sorry for themselves and deserve sympathy from others. Remember, self-pity is a character defect and not an emotion. It is choosing to feel like you're a victim when you're not.

We need to recognize the difference between a mental obsession and a genuine feeling. It is normal to grieve and to feel sadness. Self-pity however, goes further than this by replaying our being a victim in our minds. We can then use this to justify anything to ourselves. This is the great danger of self-pity.

If something bad happens in our life, it is normal to feel sadness. We need to feel the emotion for what it really is and work through the sadness. We need to make sure that we don't play a mental game of self-pity with emotion. We must not take whatever events that caused the sadness and turn it into a mental obsession. If we do, then we are headed down the road of self-pity and possibly a relapse.

Enabling another person's self-pity in recovery can have a disastrous outcome. By offering sympathy, we may only set them up to fail. A person in recovery is not only trying to heal their body, but also their emotional state of mind. When they start acting like emotionally secure adults, then eventually, hopefully the mind will follow.

One of the sayings we hear in meetings is, *"Poor me, pour me a drink."* Self-pity is feeling sorry for yourself while you forget what you have to be grateful for. Take a look around the rooms and you probably won't have to look too far to find someone else who is a lot worse off than you. This is a major key in fighting self-pity. If we can maintain any gratitude at all, then it is nearly impossible to feel sorry for ourselves.

There are a number of other ways to see gratitude in our lives. We can start by thanking God for the things we have in our life, such as our family, friends, health, employment etc. And by all means we must not forget our gift of being sober. When we acknowledge that God can replace self-pity with gratitude, then we can begin to turn this defect over to Him.

The solution is to realize that our unhappiness is caused by our self-centeredness. When we are continually focused on ourselves, it comes at the price of excluding others. This self-absorption is like a block wall around us that keeps out those who can help us.

We have to take the focus off of ourselves and begin to see that there are those around us who also have trials and struggles in their lives. We can be someone they can lean on. As we open up and start to reach out to help others, they in turn can help us.

Another way out of self-pity is through forgiveness. We aren't only talking about the forgiveness of others, but also the forgiveness of self. As we begin to forgive others of the perceived hurts and wrongs they have committed towards us, we can begin to heal and let go of the pain and self-pity. Is this easy you ask? Not by a long shot! Is it necessary? Absolutely!

We need also to remember to forgive ourselves. For so many years we have beat ourselves up to the point of self-hatred. This behavior has totally destroyed our self-worth. We need to realize that if we don't recognize the effects that it has on us, then we will never be able to start the healing process.

Helen Keller once said, *"Self-pity is our worst enemy and if we yield to it, we can never do anything good in the world."*

Anger

The third deadly sin is near the top of the list of character flaws discussed in AA meetings. It competes with fear for the top position. Anger is a feeling of strong displeasure turned against anyone or anything that we believe has hurt or wronged others or ourselves.

Recognizing and being able to channel anger is one of the greatest challenges for any recovering alcoholic. Dry drunks or relapses are often related to the inability for us to express anger properly. Uncontrolled anger is always a threat to the recovery of a newcomer as well as the long-timer. We need to be able to identify our anger signs and the causes. We need to know how to react and also learn how to prevent and prepare for situations rather than get angry about them.

Let's take a look at how the Twelve Steps can help us with anger problems. Then maybe we will be able to help identify and keep our anger from doing any further damage to us or others.

The First Step can help us to recognize and express our anger. By simply admitting we are powerless to control what, when and where we feel angry. We will get a better awareness of our feelings. We have no more control over any feelings of getting mad, sad or glad, than we do of wanting a drink. We admit to the unmanageability we feel when we get angry. This is the first step in admitting that we definitely need help to address our anger problems.

After this admission of powerlessness, we come to believe that a Power greater than ourselves can lead us to expressing our feelings in a healthier manner.

In the Third Step, we don't necessarily turn our feelings over to God as much as the attempt to control them by denying them. God gave us these feelings and He wants us to experience them for what they are. They are part of our natural make-up of human desires and instincts.

The Fourth Step helps us inventory the past and how we dealt with and reacted to our feelings of anger. We should discuss this with our sponsors in depth and admit to him or her the exact cause and effect of our anger. We need to remember that anger is only one of several symptoms of emotional insecurity that will keep us from the freedom of self that we are seeking.

When we come to the Sixth and Seventh Steps, it is very important that we understand that anger is not a character defect. Anger is a normal, God given feeling. What we do or don't do with that feeling will bring out any of our defects. Denying anger, blaming and the manipulation of others are only a few character defects that result from not dealing with our anger properly. We become willing to have God remove these defects and we humbly ask Him to do so. We are not asking God to take away our feelings. We are asking Him to take away any of the negative reactions caused by our anger.

The Tenth Step asks us to continue our inventory. This can simply entail a spot check on how we are feeling now. Asking ourselves, *"How do I feel right now?"* This helps us become more aware of how subtle our feelings connect us to others and situations that pop-up around us.

Through prayer and meditation which is suggested in the Eleventh Step, we seek out guidance from others and our Higher Power on how best to deal with anger. As we start to become more aware of our own feelings, we experience a more heightened sense of life. Anger helps us to see what we like or don't like. It also makes us take a look at who we are, what we have become and who we want to be.

Step Twelve is not only the message we carry to others on how we stopped drinking through our experience, strength and hope. But also the message of how we have found out much more about ourselves and our feelings of being able to live in balance with others.

How should we react to anger? We start by changing our thoughts for example; *"I'm angry at you because you..."* to; *"It's unfortunate this happened, but it's not worth the price I will pay."* Stop the blame game! Talk directly to the person involved or, better yet talk to your sponsor first. Use a calm and assertive voice. Practice listening and don't think of what you are going to say next. If you are thinking of what you want to say, then you can't hear what the other person is saying. Don't interrupt! Be as polite as you would want someone to be to you. If you are too angry to talk to the person, then practice Step Ten and step back and assess what is going on. Collect your thoughts and let God speak through you. It is often best not to say whatever is on your mind. While it is important to express anger, taking the time to find a respectful yet honest approach to represent your feelings will work much better.

Name calling is simply being immature and childish. The end result is likely to be destructive. Stomping out the door or hanging up on someone doesn't accomplish anything positive either. If you need to leave or end a conversation so as not to say something negative, excuse yourself without blaming the other person. Try to use a statement such as; *"Please excuse me. I am afraid I will say something that I may regret later."* Tell the other person when you will return, such as; *"I am going to take a walk to calm myself down and we can talk when I come back in a hour, ok?"* Be sure you get a response, or you may return to someone who is still pissed off at you.

Dry Drunk

Dry drunk is a term that should never be used when someone is having a bad day or when life throws us a curve. Ups and downs that everyone experiences shouldn't be labeled to be anything more than what they truly are. The dry drunk is a condition far more serious than the highs and lows of our day-to-day life.

The word intoxication comes from the Greek word for poison. Dry drunk only implies it as being a state of mind and that it is poisonous to the alcoholic's well being.

A person that is experiencing a dry drunk appears to have removed themselves from sobriety. The alcoholic for what ever reason they have given has failed to accept the necessary conditions for living a sober life. They may never have applied this principle of living in the first place. Their mental and emotional thoughts and actions are in chaos. And their approach to everyday living is unrealistic. Their destructive behavior, which may have become both verbal or physical is totally unacceptable.

There are many conditions that have tell tail signs of someone who is experiencing a dry drunk. Let's take a look at the following examples. The seventh promise of sobriety; *"Self seeking will slip away,"* basically tells us that grandiosity needs to go. This promise becomes one of the benefits of sobriety when we have become aware that we have made spiritual progress.

Before we got sober, we always said that our drinking wasn't anyone's business. Our whole attitude put us on the defensive. We thought that we had to protect our right to be who we thought we were. So for us to be self-seeking, self-indulgent and self-centered seemed only justified to us.

In sobriety though, we have come to realize that by being self-centered, we only created a denial that kept us from surrendering. We realized just how much help we really needed.

It seemed for many of us that it wasn't only natural while we were drinking to want to feed our egos, but it was also entertaining. Having this ego only allowed us very little room for character growth. If there were any chance for change it was restrained by lack of well needed humility.

At first we maybe saw self-seeking as only an inferiority complex turned inside out. As our self-centeredness began to slip away, humility starts to enter. As our self-seeking diminishes, humility allowed us to listen. Arrogant people are not willing to listen, even when they know they are wrong. If we aren't able to hear, we won't be able to grow.

Change is a must for us and without it we can not take the vital inventories that identify our defects. Without change, old ideas will continue to rule our lives. All change must come from within us directed by a Higher Power. The results will depend on how much we want to change. How hard are we willing to work and how open to advice from our sponsors and others are we willing to be?

Intolerance leaves no room for delaying the gratification of one's personal desires. This is merely misdirection of our priorities that mistakenly have given more importance to our personal needs.

Impulsiveness is the result of intolerance or the lack of ability to delay gratification of one's desires. This impulsiveness is described as any behavior which shows a reckless disregard for the ultimate consequence for self or others.

Being indecisive is closely related to impulsiveness. It

takes no accountability of the consequences of our actions. Indecisiveness is an exaggeration of the negative effects of the action. When one can't make up their mind between two or more possible courses of action, more times than not, nothing will change.

These conditions or defects of grandiosity, intolerance, impulsiveness and indecisiveness when taken separately or together, can lead to other unhealthy outcomes such as mood swings. An alcoholic will zero in on what they want others to think is the cause of their mood swing, when in fact it has nothing to do with it at all. More often that not it is something much deeper.

Introspection is a very healthy thing to do. Although it is very difficult for the dry drunk to accomplish. It means to look inward and to examine one's thoughts and desires which are directly related to one's attitude.

Detachment is an act of not caring one way or another. It is having no likes or dislikes and ultimately withdrawing from any decision making. Not wanting to have any confrontation at all may seem to be the easier, softer way out, but eventually you will need to address what is at hand.

Romanticism may be something that will set in. A kind of yearning for the past, such as freedom from care that may be associated with drinking buddies. Maybe the sounds of certain music or songs. Past relationships or even the clinking of ice cubes in a glass might be all it takes.

The term dry drunk therefore shows us that there is no change in the attitude and behavior of the alcoholic that might have regressed from a period of successful sobriety. It has become more apparent that the alcoholic is experiencing more than just a few ups and downs.

The alcoholic will rationalize their own irresponsible

behavior and almost always they will find fault in others. Although not denying their own shortcomings, they will attempt to escape being noticed by pointing out in great detail other people's faults.

Another maneuver of a dry drunk is over-reaction. They may try to attach a seemingly disproportionate intensity of feeling to an ordinary insignificant event or mishap.

Some who experience the dry drunk seem to have all the answers. They are very seldom at a loss for words when it comes to self-diagnosis.

It will be obvious for those around them that their growth has limited them in all areas. Their maturity levels will seem adolescent. They will lack the spontaneity that sober alcoholics have. Their life may feel like the walls are closing in around them. Their attitudes and behaviors are repetitive and seemingly very predictable.

Alcoholics must learn early in sobriety that humility and a power greater than themselves is what will guide them to be able to form a productive sober life. A measure of self-discipline must accompany their ego deflation process. What is needed is self-discipline through honesty, patience and responsibility towards the recovery process, along with a total acceptance of their disease.

To improve any long term goals of sobriety they must be aware of mental triggers. They need to get more involved in their recovery program. Get active in the Twelve Steps. Not only get a sponsor, but use their sponsor. Most of all they will need to pass the message along to another alcoholic who is still suffering.

Hopefully they will begin to fully appreciate the fact that their life has become somewhat manageable again. They find that sanity is possible and that it is being slowly restored. They may see that turning their lives over to a power that is greater than them isn't really that difficult.

They may see that personal inventories are not needed as often. Since they are not continuing to make the wrong decisions, they are no longer subject to the embarrassing need of repairing the wrongs that they have done.

We can only hope that when a dry drunk awakens to the irony that their life is still unmanageable and that they are still powerless, they will feel sufficiently desperate to want to change. But this can only be accomplished if they follow the path of the simple program of Alcoholics Anonymous.

Complacency

Many of us who make it through the first few years of recovery and who have been working the steps the best way we were taught, realize we now have a new problem to be concerned with. That problem is complacency! A lot of the old-timers will tell you that this is the number one offender for those who have relapsed. We can see the evidence of this when we hear people describe how they did relapse after a period of sobriety. They don't talk so much about a resentment that took them back out. Instead, they usually are so baffled that at first they can't figure out why they even picked up a drink at all. They only know that they did. They don't even realize that they drifted away from meetings or even started to let up on recovery in general.

Keep in mind we aren't talking about the loafers, slippers, sneakers or flip flops that never really seem to fit comfortably into the shoes of sobriety. We are talking about men and women with multiple years of sobriety. People who had turned the AA principles into a way of life. These were people who chose to stop growing, maybe without even realizing it. They stopped doing all the basic things that gave them the life they had been searching for in the first place.

Most of us find out after the fact of going through the pain and suffering of a relapse, that it was the little things that slowly ate away at us. This kept us from continuing spiritual progress. Complacency set in when we got too comfortable in our recovery. We started to believe the lie that after so many years of being sober, we shouldn't have to go to so many meetings or let alone work with a sponsor. We didn't stay active in service or work with newcomers. All of these things and more are the most effective tools for defeating complacency in the long run. Helping other alcoholics can only strengthen our gift and ensure us continual progress.

It seems obvious that we want to stay vigilant and fight complacency so that we can remain sober over the long haul. One of the things that will help us accomplish this is to have a home group. People in a home group can get to know us better than we know ourselves. They will call us on the things we will justify in our minds. They know when we are having a bad day and can help us get through it. They want to help because it helps them also.

What about sponsorship? If we don't use a sponsor to keep guiding us, then we most definitely are doomed. The rooms are filled with people who think that just because they went through the steps that they don't need to have as much contact with their sponsors. This is so far from the truth! Most of us in the first year or two, after having gone through the steps, still haven't got a clue of who we really are.

These things we are talking about aren't new to us. But we do have to remember that we have a built in forgetter. It may take a while, but in time we will forget how bad it really was out there and just how much pain we really were in. This is why it is so vital for us to keep listening to the newcomer. They remind us where we don't want to end up again.

Unless we continue to be vigilant through discovering self through humility, honesty, self-regulation and spiritual reliance on a daily basis, we will soon find ourselves raising our hands as a newcomer again. That is if we make it back at all.

Being vigilant and staying active in the program is how we recover from complacency. Here is a list of some other examples that will help keep us from getting lazy in recovery. We can start changing our fears into a strong faith through courage. We can turn our hate into love. Deflating our egos will give us some humility. By giving anxiety and worry to serenity we gain peace of mind. Turn our denial into acceptance, our jealousy into trust, our fantasies into reality, selfishness into service, resentment into forgiveness, being judgmental into tolerance, despair into hope, self-hate into self-respect, and loneliness into fellowship. Working on anyone of the above is a motivator to keep us from getting complacent.

You learned all of this when you went through the steps the first time. If you didn't, then you were either not honest with yourself and your sponsor or you never worked the steps in the first place. You know what the truth is. If you did learn these life saving principles and still went back out, it is not to late to save your life again. Through doing these simple suggestions of the program you will learn again to understand all of the principles and ultimately through God's grace you will live a long, sober life.

Emotional Sobriety

For most of us our emotions seem to be either on or off. We either feel too little or too much. We loose our ability to fine tune and stay within a medium range of balance. We tend to start living on emotional edges rather than in middle grounds.

Emotions impact our thinking more than our thinking impacts our emotions. When our emotions are out of control, then so is our thinking. If we can't bring our feelings and thinking into some sort of balance, then our life and our relationships will show it.

Emotional sobriety is all about finding and maintaining this balance. It's about the even keel that helps us to adjust the intensity of our emotional responses to life situations. Emotional sobriety is having the ability to bring ourselves into balance when we fall.

Good self-regulation can help us in literally every part of life, from our relationships with other people to the amount of food we eat or even how much sleep we get. These powerful emotions can smother our thoughts and make it difficult for us to use any reason to bring our emotions back into balance.

When we maintain good self-regulation, we are able to manage the daily ups and downs of life and relationships without going off on someone. We also are not shutting down or withdrawing and making irrational decisions with later regrets. We seem to have more resilience. We can concentrate better, whether we are trying to hang on to a conversation, having a lousy day or any emotionally stressful situation. We can use our thinking to lead us to emotional clarity and understanding, because our emotions are staying within a range that we can tolerate.

It's all about living in an emotional balance so that we are in a better position to enjoy our lives. We can feel passionate and yes, know when we are not in tune so we can figure out what we need to do to get back where we are comfortable.

In an effort to improve a state of emotional sobriety, it is imperative to increase the number of AA meetings we go to. Through the years we hear too many stories of other members in AA picking up the drink after going through situations such as job loss, death, financial insecurity and breakups. AA meetings are some of the only places on the planet where a person can go, to openly verbalize and share their concerns, issues and problems with groups of other people, without the fear of being shunned, laughed at or rejected. We shouldn't forget to bring theses same problems to our sponsors first.

Another reason for going to our sponsors first is to insure we don't cause anymore damage to others and also to ourselves, especially when an amends is involved.

We find it to be true, that even after years of sobriety it was our best thinking that got us here. Our thoughts still will get us into trouble unless we are in balance physically, emotionally, mentally and spiritually.

How many times have we had an idea and shared it at a meeting or openly with someone and have been left with that nauseating feeling in our stomachs asking ourselves, *"Why on earth did I say that?"* The action in this case would to have been to impose my thoughts, without prior investigation on someone else and expect a result. And when the result did not happen the way I thought it should have, my emotional balance would be shaken whether I saw it then or not.

Perhaps it would be a lot easier to list some behaviors

and situations of emotional sobriety that are lacking, than it would be to list examples of successful emotional sobriety. Some that AA members frequently demonstrate that may show the need for improvement. Some areas that may need work are excessive anger, jealousy, sexual fantasy, neediness, smothering, delusions of grandeur and self-pity.

Alcoholics by nature have a craving for instant gratification of which others cannot identify with. It is only logical that they would also want and expect instant improvement within their emotional sobriety. For members of AA, that improvement does not come quickly or easily. In most alcoholic's humble opinion, the best way to achieve emotional sobriety is to communicate regularly with their sponsors, do step work, share at meetings and work with others. Emotional sobriety is an often elusive, hard to define concept or state of mind that is so vital to the quality of life for many in recovery.

We are responsible for our feelings! People, places and situations don't make us angry. We allow ourselves to get angry. Why would we let someone live rent free in our heads? If we are not willing to let someone or some situation put our physical sobriety at risk, then why would it be any different to put any less value on our emotional sobriety?

We had to give up the booze to obtain physical sobriety. For emotional sobriety we must stop blaming others. We must do away with our expectations of others. We must accept responsibility for our lives, our actions and our emotions. Circumstances don't determine the quality of our sobriety. The quality of our sobriety is determined by our reactions to circumstances.

My Story

(published in August 2010 issue of The Grape Vine)

My sobriety date is May 9th 2003. This however is not my first time in AA. I was introduced to the program in 1982 in Cincinnati, Ohio. My older brother took me to my first meeting when I was twenty three years old. My next meeting would not be until November of 1985 in Santa Barbara, Ca.

When I was in that meeting in Ohio I had no idea what those people were talking about and I really could have cared less. I knew I certainly didn't belong there. They sounded pretty screwed up. I was more worried about who and where I was going to party with next. But, I sat with my brother because he said he needed to be there.

At that time in my life I had messed things up really good. I left my first wife and son for her best friend. My son had just turned three. The affair lasted a couple of months and she went back to her husband.

I couldn't face my family and I ran. I didn't realize how much damage and pain I had caused them until years later after I got sober. In the mean time I kept running and always getting into trouble. This seemed to be a pattern since I was about twelve years old. Always in trouble due to alcohol and getting arrested more times than I can remember and never realizing that alcohol was the main ingredient.

This way of life took me to places I never wanted to end up in. I had changed my name because of being on the run from the law. I was afraid to get a job because I would be found. I lived on the road and ended up stealing or selling drugs to make a living. When the fear of being caught stealing was too much, I started robbing drug dealers. I figured they wouldn't be filing any complaints and the thought of them killing me didn't scare me.

My alcohol and drug addiction was costing me around $100.00 a day. Coke and pot happened to be my other seat on the Titanic and even though I was sinking fast, it seemed like life kept throwing me life lines to survive. The next life line was becoming a bartender. This was my free ticket to coke. After all, when you are in charge of all the liquor that can be drunk, who wouldn't want to be your friend?

Living in the fast lane was exciting, but it was also talking a toll on my health. There were days when my blood felt like pure alcohol. I am sure I had alcohol poisoning on several occasions. One day after what seemed like a life time of insanity, I remember waking up in the emergency room. The doctor told me that I had a drug induced stroke or a TIA. This had sent me into a catatonic state. I had lost some sight in my left eye and was partially paralyzed in my left arm. Through my denial I still was trying to convince the doctor that it must be a brain tumor. My denial was at it's peak. He suggested I check into a treatment center for alcohol and drug abuse. I told him that I probably did need a rest.

Convincing myself that I graduated from that thirty day program, I realized I knew everything there was to know about getting sober. So I did what any good alcoholic would do. I went out and celebrated! I forgot how bad detox sucks. It was as if I had never stopped drinking. Actually it was worse. Alcohol again had literally taken me to within inches of my life. It was then that I realized and admitted not only was I scared for the first time in my life, but that I had a serious problem that I could not control. The only place left was AA.

My life was really messed up! For the past few years I had been living under an alias name. Looking back over my life, I had been locked up a dozen times in five different states. I had ruined any relationship including family. I hadn't spoken with my son in six or seven years. Now I had taken another hostage in marriage. By the grace of God she has been sober ever since.

After I got out of detox again I did get into action. I got a sponsor and followed most of his suggestions. I worked the steps the best I could. To my amazement the obsession to drink was taken away. When my mind began to clear a little, after maybe a few months, I realized that my family hadn't heard from me for several years. In fact the last time they new I was alive was when I made the newspapers a few years prior in Florida, New York, Arkansas, Tennessee and California simultaneously.

I had done so much damage that I didn't know where to begin. Thank God the steps are in order for a reason! Thank God for sponsorship! My sponsor walked me through the next five and a half years the best he could. I know today that I was not living sober then. I was a dry drunk on a collision course for relapse and didn't even realize it.

I had been battling depression I thought. First it was the divorce from my second wife that I got sober with. This mainly was due to my lack of honesty. I blamed her for a long time for my insane actions. This justification ended up being a resentment that nearly killed me. I then moved back to Florida to be near my family and try to be a father to my son who I had seen once in eight years. My motives were well intended, but my priorities were way out of balance.

Cunning, baffling, powerful and patient! I started listening to the lies that my disease was telling me. It told me that if I just stayed away from the drugs that I would be okay. It said I didn't fit into AA in this area and that the AA here wasn't any good. It had me convinced that I knew enough about sobriety and that I could stay sober on my own. Within three months I was slamming down the brews, pounding on the bar and wondering how the hell did this happen to me again.

Today I know how this happened. When I moved back to Florida I didn't seek out meetings. I went to a few, but I didn't feel comfortable. I didn't get a sponsor and didn't stay in contact with anyone I got sober with. When I lost the two jobs I had, someone offered me a beer and I took it. This was the last lie that I bought into. It told me that I might as well drink because things couldn't get any worse.

My ego and pride kept me from coming back for the next twelve years. Not a day went by that I drew a sober breath. I used to wonder how I ever made it through those years. Today I know that God had a different plan for me. He really does take care of fools and drunks and I was definitely both.

I had been in the jungles of Colombia, South America on and off for about three years mining gold with my oldest brother. When I was there my drinking was at it's most dangerous point. From drinking in the barrios of Medellin, Cali and many other places, to knocking out an agent for their secret police in San Andres. I was ordered to leave the island the next morning before the agent could find me. It really is another story by it's self.

Not long after I got back I took another hostage in marriage. After about six years she was all but done with me. She was always afraid to come home to an angry drunk. I was afraid to come home one day because I thought I had spent all the money in the bank. I didn't know she had changed the accounts and was getting ready to have me thrown out. I had made her a prisoner in her own home. How could this be happening to me?

As I sat out on the back porch with a gun in my mouth and listening to the disease screaming at me, telling me that this was the only way out, I heard a voice within me say, "You need to get back to AA." My dad told me that before he died. He told me that all of us need fellowship whether it comes from church or in my case he said AA. He explained to me that my spirit was broken and lost and the only way to find it again was to ask God for direction. He had died on October 19th 2002. It wasn't until May 8th 2003 the same day on the porch when I was praying at his grave that I heard that voice again say "you need to get sober." This time the voice was so loud, that I looked around to see if someone was actually there. It seemed like I cried for hours. I don't question whether it was my dad or God speaking to me. I do accept the fact that this was my spiritual awakening. When I told my wife that I was going back to AA, all she said was thank you.

The next day I walked thru the doors of AA again. Since that day I have had many spiritual experiences. Some were so small that in the beginning I used to take them for granted, thinking that they were only coincidences.

The depression that I thought I had when I was in AA before was not depression at all. I know today it was a dry drunk. I was living a life of lies and trying to work a program of honesty.

Today my life is awesome! Chaotic at times, but awesome! My wife and I celebrated our fourteenth wedding anniversary in 2010. I have a strong loving relationship with my son and granddaughter. I have a younger daughter that I haven't seen for thirteen years and she wants to finally meet me. The brother that took me to my first meeting is sober today.

Due to the twelve steps and good friends that I have come to love, I have zero resentment in my life most of the time. If I choose to acquire one, I have many tools to release it. I am more humble today because I have faced my past humiliations and fears. I am able to recognize most of my emotions whether they are healthy or unhealthy ones. And if I can't see a defect, then someone in my home group or my sponsor will be glad to point it out for me.

I attend meetings weekly. Not only because I know I need to keep coming, but because I like the meetings. I like being there for someone else who is struggling. I want to continue to be teachable. If I don't remain teachable I am not able to see the changes that I need.

Today I live in the H.O.W. The steps have given me a freedom I never thought possible. Today is a great day to be sober and if God allows me the time, tomorrow will be a great day also.

This book is not meant to take the place of any of the AA literature that saved my life. My hope is that you may have heard something in my story or you read something in this book that helps you to find a sober path. If not, please call someone! There are hundreds of meetings on a daily basis within a short distance. There are hundreds of thousands of people who attend these meetings. And I can promise you that none of them want you to take a drink today and will help you anyway they can.

John C.
Palm Bay, FL.

<u>In memory of a few special people</u>

Charlie J.... always had a kind word!

Bernie D.... loved to make you laugh!

Tom A.... was always there to lend a hand!

To all the others who were always there for us!
You will never be forgotten!

<u>To some friends I've met along the way</u>

Floyd C.... Your spirituality is an inspiration!

Tom H.... For your humorous truth!

Pete M.... Your perseverance is amazing!

Pete W, George C, Bobbie B, Eva S, Beverly, Don, Dottie,
Hope, John P, B.C., Judd, Conan, Kathy & Pete M,
And to so many more, thank you for my life!

To my good friend and sponsee Brad T. love you bro!

I want to thank my family for their support and love,
especially my wife Laurie!